Illinois Learning Standards

STATE GOAL 14: Understand political systems, with an emphasis on the United States.

14.A.2 Explain the importance of fundamental concepts expressed and implied in major documents including the Declaration of Independence, the United States Constitution and the Illinois Constitution.

14.B.2 Explain what government does at local, state and national levels.

14.C.2 Describe and evaluate why rights and responsibilities are important to the individual, family, community, workplace, state and nation (e. g., voting, protection under the law).

14.D.2 Explain ways that individuals and groups influence and shape public policy.

14.E.2 Determine and explain the leadership role of the United States in international settings.

14.F.2 Identify consistencies and inconsistencies between expressed United States political traditions and ideas and actual practices (e.g., freedom of speech, right to bear arms, slavery, voting rights).

STATE GOAL 15: Understand economic systems, with an emphasis on the United States.

15.A.2a Explain how economic systems decide what goods and services are produced, how they are produced and who consumes them.

15.A.2b Describe how incomes reflect choices made about education and careers.

15.A.2c Describe unemployment.

15.B.2a Identify factors that affect how consumers make their choices.

15.B.2b Explain the relationship between the quantity of goods/services purchased and their price.

15.B.2c Explain that when a choice is made, something else is given up.

15.C.2a Describe the relationship between price and quantity supplied of a good or service.

15.C.2b Identify and explain examples of competition in the economy.

15.C.2c Describe how entrepreneurs take risks in order to produce goods or services.

15.D.2a Explain why people and countries voluntarily exchange goods and services.

15.D.2b Describe the relationships among specialization, division of labor, productivity of workers and interdependence among producers and consumers.

15E.2a Explain how and why public goods and services are provided.

15.E.2b Identify which public goods and services are provided by differing levels of government.

STATE GOAL 16: Understand events, trends, individuals and movements shaping the history of Illinois, the United States and other nations.

16.A.2a Read historical stories and determine events which influenced their writing.

16.A.2b Compare different stories about a historical figure or event and analyze differences in the portrayals and perspectives they present.

16.A.2c Ask questions and seek answers by collecting and analyzing data from historic documents, images and other literary and non-literary sources.

16.B.2a (US) Describe how the European colonies in North America developed politically.

16.B.2b (US) Identify major causes of the American Revolution and describe the consequences of the Revolution through the early national period, including the roles of George Washington, Thomas Jefferson and Benjamin Franklin.

16.B.2c (US) Identify presidential elections that were pivotal in the formation of modern political parties.

16.B.2d (US) Identify major political events and leaders within the United States historical eras since the adoption of the Constitution, including the westward expansion, Louisiana Purchase, Civil War, and 20th century wars as well as the roles of Thomas Jefferson, Abraham Lincoln, Woodrow Wilson, and Franklin D. Roosevelt.

16.B.2a (W) Describe the historical development of monarchies, oligarchies and city-states in ancient civilizations.

16.B.2b (W) Describe the origins of Western political ideas and institutions (e.g. Greek democracy, Roman republic, Magna Carta and Common Law, the Enlightenment).

16.C.2a (US) Describe how slavery and indentured servitude influenced the early economy of the United States.

16.C.2b (US) Explain how individuals, including John Deere, Thomas ~~~~~~~~ McCormack, George Washin~~~~~~~~~~~~~~~~ontributed to econor~~~~~~~~~~~~~~~~~~~~ and entrep~~~~~~

16.C.2c (US) Describe significant economic events including industrialization, immigration, the Great Depression, the shift to a service economy and the rise of technology that influenced history from the industrial development era to the present.

16.C.2a (W) Describe the economic consequences of the first agricultural revolution, 4000 BCE-1000 BCE.

16.C.2b (W) Describe the basic economic systems of the world's great civilizations including Mesopotamia, Egypt, Aegean/Mediterranean and Asian civilizations, 1000 BCE - 500 CE.

16.C.2c (W) Describe basic economic changes that led to and resulted from the manorial agricultural system, the industrial revolution, the rise of the capitalism and the information/communication revolution.

16.D.2a (US) Describe the various individual motives for settling in colonial America.

16.D.2b (US) Describe the ways in which participation in the westward movement affected families and communities.

16.D.2c US) Describe the influence of key individuals and groups, including Susan B. Anthony/suffrage and Martin Luther King, Jr./civil rights, in the historical eras of Illinois and the United States.

16.D.2 (W) Describe the various roles of men, women and children in the family, at work, and in the community in various time periods and places (e.g., ancient Rome, Medieval Europe, ancient China, Sub-Saharan Africa).

16.E.2a (US) Identify environmental factors that drew settlers to the state and region.

16.E.2b US) Identify individuals and events in the development of the conservation movement including John Muir, Theodore Roosevelt and the creation of the National Park System.

16.E.2c (US) Describe environmental factors that influenced the development of transportation and trade in Illinois.

16.E.2a (W) Describe how people in hunting and gathering and early pastoral societies adapted to their respective environments.

16.E.2b (W) Identify individuals and their inventions (e.g. Watt/ steam engine, Nobel/TNT, Edison/electric light) which influenced world environmental history.

STATE GOAL 17: Understand world geography and the effects of geography on society, with an emphasis on the United States.

17.A.2a Compare the physical characteristics of places including soils, land forms, vegetation, wildlife, climate, natural hazards.

17.A.2b Use maps and other geographic representations and instruments to gather information about people, places and environments.

17.B.2a Describe how physical and human processes shape spatial patterns including erosion, agriculture and settlement.

17.B.2b Explain how physical and living components interact in a variety of ecosystems including desert, prairie, flood plain, forest, tundra.

17.C.2a Describe how natural events in the physical environment affect human activities.

17.C.2b Describe the relationships among location of resources, population distribution and economic activities (e.g., transportation, trade, communications).

17.C.2c Explain how human activity affects the environment.

17.D.2a Describe how physical characteristics of places influence people's perceptions and their roles in the world over time.

17.D.2b Identify different settlement patterns in Illinois and the United States and relate them to physical features and resources.

STATE GOAL 18: Understand social systems, with an emphasis on the United States.

18.A.2 Explain ways in which language, stories, folk tales, music, media and artistic creations serve as expressions of culture.

18.B.2a Describe interactions of individuals, groups and institutions in situations drawn from the local community (e.g., local response to state and national reforms).

18.B.2b Describe the ways in which institutions meet the needs of society.

18.C.2 Describe how changes in production (e.g., hunting and gathering, agricultural, industrial) and population caused changes in social systems.

ILLINOIS
Macmillan/McGraw-Hill TIMELINKS

Illinois and Our Nation

PROGRAM AUTHORS
James A. Banks
Kevin P. Colleary
Linda Greenow
Walter C. Parker
Emily M. Schell
Dinah Zike

CONTRIBUTORS
Raymond C. Jones
Irma M. Olmedo

 Macmillan/McGraw-Hill

Volume 2

PROGRAM AUTHORS

James A. Banks, Ph.D.
Kerry and Linda Killinger
  Professor of Diversity Studies
  and Director, Center for
  Multicultural Education
University of Washington
Seattle, Washington

Kevin P. Colleary, Ed.D.
Curriculum and Teaching
  Department
Graduate School of Education
Fordham University
New York, New York

Linda Greenow, Ph.D.
Associate Professor and Chair
Department of Geography
State University of New York at
  New Paltz
New Paltz, New York

Walter C. Parker, Ph.D.
Professor of Social Studies
  Education, Adjunct Professor
  of Political Science
University of Washington
Seattle, Washington

Emily M. Schell, Ed.D.
Visiting Professor, Teacher
  Education
San Diego State University
San Diego, California

Dinah Zike
Educational Consultant
Dinah-Mite Activities, Inc.
San Antonio, Texas

CONTRIBUTORS

Raymond C. Jones, Ph.D.
Director of Secondary Social
  Studies Education
Wake Forest University
Winston-Salem, North Carolina

Irma M. Olmedo
Associate professor
University of Illinois-Chicago
College of Education
Chicago, Illinois

HISTORIANS/SCHOLARS

Ned Blackhawk
Associate Professor of History
  and American Indian Studies
University of Wisconsin
Madison, Wisconsin

Sheilah F. Clarke-Ekong, Ph.D.
Professor of Anthropology
University of Missouri-St. Louis
St. Louis, Missouri

Larry Dale, Ph.D.
Director, Center for Economic
  Education
Arkansas State University
Jonesboro, Arkansas

Brooks Green, Ph.D.
Associate Professor of
  Geography
University of Central Arkansas
Conway, Arkansas

Thomas C. Holt, Ph.D.
Professor of History
University of Chicago
Chicago, Illinois

Students with print disabilities may be eligible to obtain an accessible, audio version of the pupil edition of this textbook. Please call Recording for the Blind & Dyslexic at 1-800-221-4792 for complete information.

Copyright © 2009 by The McGraw-Hill Companies, Inc. All rights reserved. Except as permitted under the United States Copyright Act, no part of this publication may be reproduced or distributed in any form or by any means, or stored in a database or retrieval system, without prior permission of the publisher.

Send all inquires to:
Macmillan/McGraw-Hill
8787 Orion Place
Columbus, OH 43240-4027

MHID 0-02-152327-4
ISBN 978-0-02-152327-6
Printed in the United States of America.
2 3 4 5 6 7 8 9 10   027/043   13 12 11 10 09 08

Illinois and Our Nation

CONTENTS, Volume 2

EXPLORE The Big Idea What causes a state to change?

Unit 5 The Story of Illinois 193

How do people and events shape the history and culture of a state?

Reference Section

Skills and Features

Maps

EXPLORE The Big Idea

Essential Question
How do natural resources affect a region's growth?

FOLDABLES™ Study Organizer

Draw Conclusions
Make a trifold book foldable to take notes as you read Unit 3. Label the three tabs **Geography**, **Economy**, and **People**.

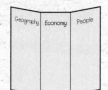

LOG ON
For more about Unit 3 go to www.macmillanmh.com

The Midwest

PEOPLE, PLACES, AND EVENTS

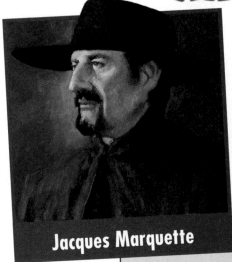

Jacques Marquette

New France

French explorers **Jacques Marquette** and Louis Jolliet explored the area of the Mississippi River in 1673. They called the area **New France**.

Today you can learn more about the Mississippi River and its explorers at the National Mississippi River Museum and Aquarium in Dubuque, Iowa..

Laura Ingalls Wilder

Wilder's Log Cabin

If you ever read a book called *Little House on the Prairie*, you read about **Laura Ingalls Wilder's** life on the frontier.

Today you can visit **Wilder's Log Cabin** in Pepin, Wisconsin.

LOG ON
For more about People, Places, and Events, visit:
www.macmillanmh.com

Lincoln Home National Historic Site

Abraham Lincoln

Our sixteenth President, **Abraham Lincoln**, lived in Springfield, Illinois. Lincoln's parents were among the first settlers to move to the Midwest.

Today you can visit the **Lincoln Home National Historic Site** to learn more about Abraham Lincoln.

The Great Lakes

Bill Hartwig

The Great Lakes are five gigantic lakes in the Midwest. **Bill Hartwig** of the National Wildlife Refuge System is one of the many people who work to keep the Great Lakes clean.

Today the Great Lakes are the largest group of freshwater lakes in the world. They're so big you can see them from space!

Midwest Region

Midwest

The Midwest is home to both important and fun places to visit.

1 Mount Rushmore honors Presidents Washington, Jefferson, T. Roosevelt, and Lincoln. Each head is about 60 feet tall.

0   100   200 kilometers

kawea

ND
Bismarck ★

SD

Lake Oahe

1 BLACK HILLS   Pierre ★

BADLANDS

N
W   E
S

NE

KS

Arkansas River

5 The American Bison was very important to Native Americans. Today there are about 350,000 in the United States.

2 Cheese and other dairy products are a very important part of the economy of the Midwest.

3 Some say that the giant footsteps of Paul Bunyan and his blue ox, Babe, created Minnesota's 10,000 lakes.

5

MESABI RANGE

Tettegouche State Park

Lake Superior

Keweenaw Peninsula

Apostle Islands National Lakeshore

UPPER PENINSULA

3

MN

SUPERIOR UPLAND

Lake Huron

Lake Ontario

St. Paul ★

Mississippi River

WI **2**

LOWER PENINSULA

Lake Michigan

MI

Lansing ★ Detroit •

Lake Erie

★ Madison

G R E A T

IA

CENTRAL PLAINS

Chicago •

P L A I N S

ALLEGHENY PLATEAU

★ Des Moines

Platte River

OH

Missouri River

★ Lincoln

IL

Wabash River

IN **4**

★ Columbus

MO

★ Springfield

★ Indianapolis

Ohio River

★ Topeka

Wayne National Forest

★ St. Louis

Jefferson City ★

Ohio River

4 The Indianapolis 500 is one of the most famous car races in the world.

INTERIOR PLAINS

OZARK PLATEAU

Mark Twain National Forest

ethanol

17

133

Lesson 1

VOCABULARY
fertile p. 136

prairie p. 138

READING SKILL
Draw Conclusions
Copy the chart. Use it to
draw conclusions about
the Mississippi River.

Text Clues	Conclusion

Illinois Learning Standards
14.D.2,16.C.2c, 16.E.2a,
17.A.2a, 17.A.2b, 17.B.2a,
17.B.2b,18.C.2,

The Geography of the Midwest

Visual Preview

How have the Great Lakes affected the Midwest?

A The Great Lakes make a good home for plants and animals.

B The Midwest has many rivers that help make the soil fertile for farming.

C The Midwest has plains, hills, mountains, and badlands.

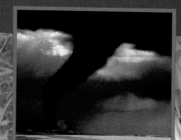

D The Midwest has hot summers, cold winters, and seasonal storms.

134

Ⓐ   A LAND FORMED BY WATER

The 12 states in the Midwest region are in the middle of the United States. This region is known as the Heartland of America. Many amazing plants and animals make this region unique and beautiful.

The Midwest region sits between the Appalachian Mountains and the Rocky Mountains. Although there are no oceans in the Midwest, there's plenty of water. Thousands of years ago, huge glaciers covered parts of the Midwest. As these gigantic sheets of ice moved slowly across the region, they flattened the land and carved out giant holes. When the glaciers melted, they filled the holes with water.

Today the holes created by the glaciers are called the Great Lakes. Lake Superior, Lake Michigan, Lake Huron, and Lake Erie are in the Midwest. Lake Ontario is in the Northeast. Thousands of smaller lakes were also formed by the glaciers. Minnesota, for example, has 22,000 lakes. All of these lakes make a good home for the region's plants and animals.

The plants and animals of the Midwest have adapted to different landforms. They have also adapted to hot summers and cold winters.

Plants and Animals of the Midwest

Foxglove Beard Tongue

White-tailed Jackrabbit

Prairie Cone Flower

Burrowing Owl

Black-eyed Susan

Red-tailed Hawk

QUICK CHECK

Draw Conclusions **Where did the water in the Great Lakes first come from?**

B FLOWING RIVERS

When the glaciers melted thousands of years ago, they created rivers. These rivers carried soil from the north and brought it south. The soil was **fertile**, or filled with vitamins and minerals that plants need to grow. Many of the states in the Midwest, such as Iowa and Ohio, now have lots of fertile soil. Fertile soil lets farmers produce crops that are healthy.

Several big rivers run through the region. More than half of the Mississippi River is in the Midwest. The Ohio River creates a southern border for Ohio, Indiana, and Illinois. The Missouri River flows into the Mississippi from the west.

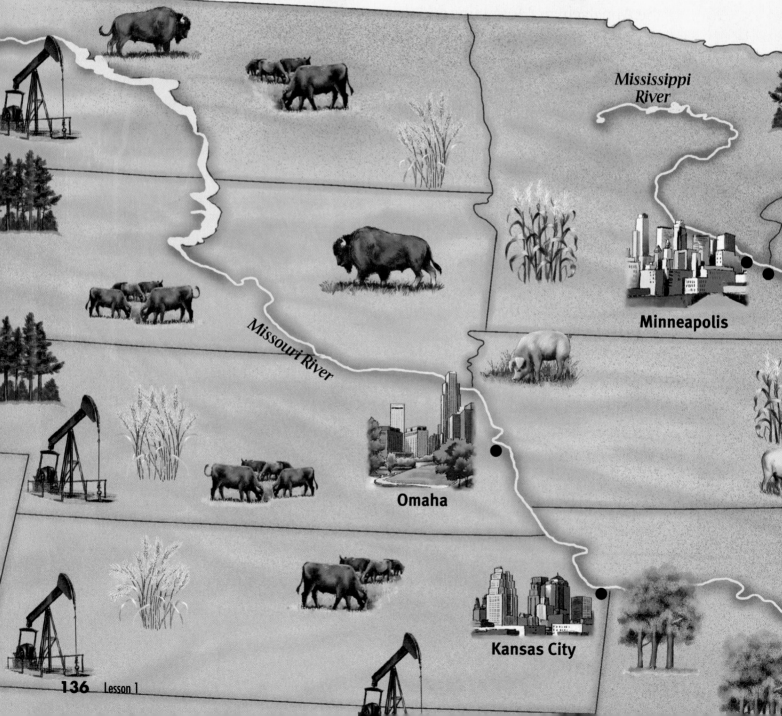

Mississippi River

Missouri River

Minneapolis

Omaha

Kansas City

PEOPLE

Samuel Clemens, also known as Mark Twain, became one of our country's best-known writers. Many of Twain's novels take place on or near the Mississippi River.

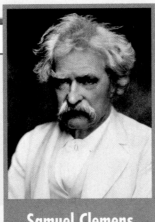

Samuel Clemens

The Missouri is more than 2,300 miles long. This river has been nicknamed the "Big Muddy" for the amount of dirt it carries in its waters. To get an idea of how much water is in the Midwest, take a look at the map below. You can see that many of the region's cities were built along river banks.

QUICK CHECK

Summarize **How did glaciers improve Midwestern soil?**

St. Paul

Cincinnati

Ohio River

Louisville

St. Louis

The Midwest is mostly flat land. There are very few hills or mountains. When glaciers moved down the region, they flattened hills and filled valleys with dirt. This created plains, or flat lands covered by grasses and wildflowers. Plains covered by grasses and wildflowers are called **prairies**.

Mountains and Hills

Glaciers didn't flatten all of the hills and mountains in the Midwest. There are hills in parts of Ohio, Michigan, and even Illinois. The farther you move away from the Great Lakes, the higher the land gets. The plains slowly give way to hills, and by the time you get as far away from the Great Lakes as you can within the region, you are in the mountains.

Harney Peak, in the Black Hills mountains of South Dakota, is 7,242 feet above sea level. Underneath the Black Hills is Wind Cave. Wind Cave has more than 100 miles of winding passages. Alvin McDonald explored the cave in the 1890s. Read about his experience below.

Primary Sources

They are still finding new rooms at the Wind Cave and we have about come to the conclusion there is no end to it.

Alvin McDonald

Write About It What did Alvin McDonald conclude about Wind Cave?

The Badlands

The Midwest has lakes, rivers, prairies, and mountains with caves. Is that all, you ask? No! There are also badlands in the Midwest. Badlands are very dry lands that have been chipped away by wind and water. The wind and water carved out canyons, ravines, gullies (narrow and deep holes that were created by water), and other such landforms. Badlands usually have a spectacular color that ranges from dark black or blue to bright red.

It just so happens that all of the badlands in the United States are in the Midwest. In North Dakota, there's Theodore Roosevelt National Park, while Badlands National Park is in South Dakota. There's also Toadstool Geologic

PLACES

Wind Cave National Park is home to one of the world's longest caves and 28,295 acres of prairie, pine forest, and diverse wildlife.

Wind Cave

Park in the Oglala National Grassland of Nebraska. Wind, water, and erosion have twisted the peaks and rocks of these badlands into unusual shapes.

QUICK CHECK

Summarize Describe the landforms of the Midwest region.

Badlands National Park, South Dakota

Tornadoes whirl around at speeds of up to 200 miles per hour.

Temperatures in the Midwest can vary widely. The areas around the Great Lakes may also experience what is called the lake effect. Since water takes longer to heat and cool than land, the air over the water is often hotter or cooler than the air over the land. When winds blow across the lakes, they carry this hot or cool air over the land, affecting the temperature.

Storms occur in the Midwest, too. In winter, heavy snowstorms whip across the plains. In summer, strong winds can form dangerous, destructive tornadoes.

QUICK CHECK

Cause and Effect How do the Great Lakes cause climate changes in the Midwest?

Check Understanding

1. VOCABULARY Summarize this lesson in a paragraph using the vocabulary words below.

fertile   prairie

2. READING SKILL Draw Conclusions Use the chart from page 134 to write a paragraph about why the Mississippi River is so large.

Text Clues	Conclusion

3. Write About It Write a paragraph about how the geography of the Midwest drew people to settle there.

Chart and Graph Skills

Compare Bar and Line Graphs

VOCABULARY

bar graph

line graph

A graph is a special kind of diagram that shows facts clearly. A **bar graph** uses bars to show information. A **line graph** shows how something has changed over time.

The bar graph below shows the value of Iowa's top five farm products in 2004. The line graph below shows how the population of the Midwest has changed.

Learn It

- Graph A is a bar graph. It shows the value of Iowa's top farm products in 2004. The height of the bars tells the value of each product in 2004.

- Graph B is a line graph. The numbers on the left of the line graph represent the population of the Midwest region. The labels at the bottom show the years that the graph covers.

Try It

- What was the population of the Midwest in 1910?

- What product had the most value in Iowa in 2004?

Apply It

- Find the number and kinds of pets your classmates have. Decide which kind of graph would be best to show the information. Make the graph.

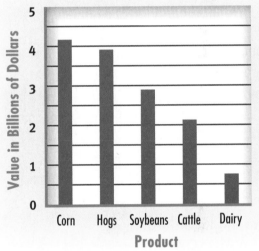

A: Iowa's Top Farm Products, 2004

Value in Billions of Dollars / Product: Corn, Hogs, Soybeans, Cattle, Dairy

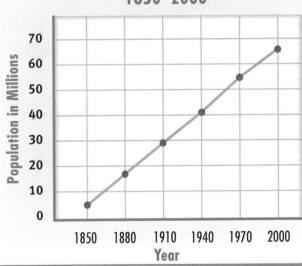

B: Population of the Midwest, 1850–2000

Population in Millions / Year: 1850, 1880, 1910, 1940, 1970, 2000

Lesson 2

VOCABULARY

iron p. 144

ore p. 144

open-pit mining p. 144

agribusiness p. 146

mass production p. 148

assembly line p. 148

READING SKILL

Draw Conclusions

Copy the chart. Use it to draw conclusions about the future of the Midwest's economy.

Text Clues	Conclusion

Illinois Learning Standards

14.E.2, 15.A.2a, 15.C.2b, 16.A.2a, 16.C.2b(US) 17.C.2c, 17.D.2a, 18.B.2b

The Economy of the Midwest

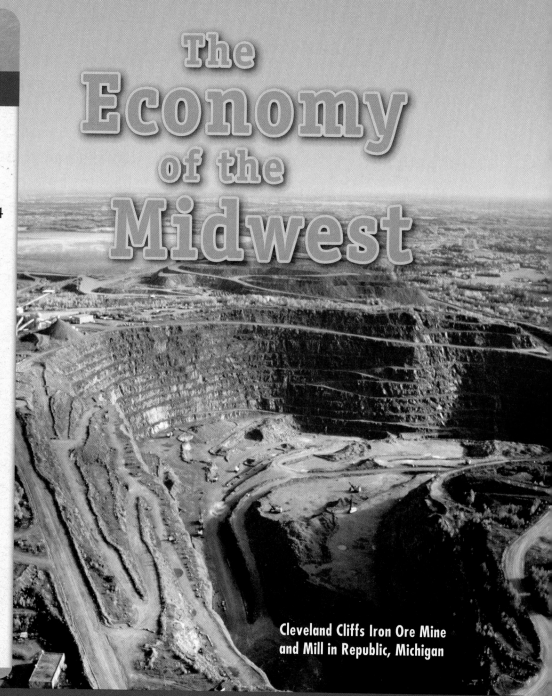

Cleveland Cliffs Iron Ore Mine and Mill in Republic, Michigan

Visual Preview

How have people made a living in the Midwest over time?

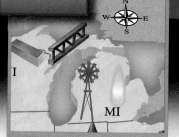

A Natural resources have always been an important part of the region's economy.

B By the 1900s, the Midwest had become a giant in steel production.

C Manufacturing and agriculture are important to the Midwest economy.

D Today the service and technology industries are important to the Midwest.

A RICH LAND

The Midwest's economy starts with the land. The land provides energy sources, such as coal, oil, and natural gas, as well as metals, such as iron and copper.

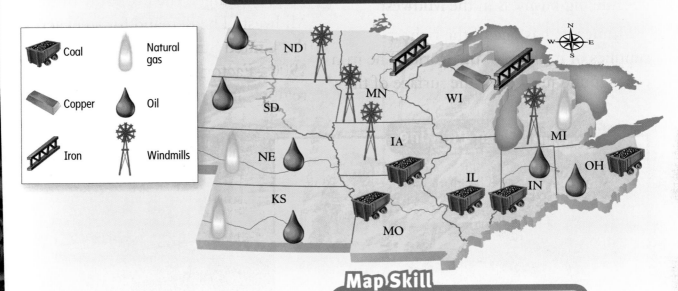

Resources of the Midwest

Coal   Natural gas

Copper   Oil

Iron   Windmills

ND, SD, MN, WI, NE, IA, MI, KS, IL, IN, OH, MO

Map Skill

LOCATION **Which states have both oil and coal as a natural resource?**

You already know that a region's economy depends heavily on the natural resources found in the region. The Midwest has many.

The region's water resources include the Great Lakes and rivers such as the Ohio, Mississippi, and Missouri. These waterways are used to ship goods across the country.

The rich soil of the Midwest provides ideal conditions for farming. When you go underground or in hills and mountains you find metals. Metals are a valuable resource.

That's not all the Midwest has. It also has wind! Strong winds that blow across the Midwest are an incredible energy source. They turn the blades of wind turbines that are used to create electricity.

QUICK CHECK

Summarize **What energy resources can be found in the Midwest?**

THE PEOPLE OF THE MIDWEST

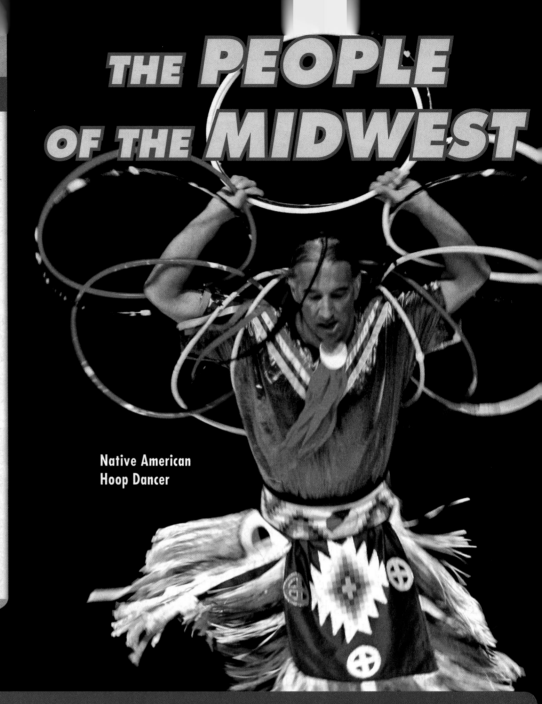

Native American
Hoop Dancer

VOCABULARY

descendants p. 151

pioneer p. 153

migration p. 153

tradition p. 155

READING SKILL

Draw Conclusions
Copy the chart. As you read, list reasons why people came to the Midwest.

Text Clues	Conclusion

Illinois Learning Standards

16.A.2c, 16.E.2c, 17.C.2b, 17.D.2b, 18.A.2, 18.B.2a, 18.B.2b, 18.C.2

Visual Preview

How have the people of the Midwest adapted to change?

A Native Americans were the first Midwesterners. Many of their mounds remain.

B Many people from Europe made the Midwest their home.

C Today immigrants to the Midwest come from all around the world.

D The Midwest is home to many great artists, musicians, writers, and athletes.

Ⓐ THE FIRST MIDWESTERNERS

Native Americans were the first people of the Midwest. Today Midwesterners are the descendants, or the children and grandchildren, of Native Americans and immigrants who have come to the Midwest from around the world.

Hundreds of years ago, a group of people that were called mound builders lived in the Midwest. They were called mound builders because they built large hills. Mound builders farmed, traded, and built cities. At one time, one of the largest Mississippian cities, Cahokia, may have had up to 20,000 people living there. The mound cultures disappeared sometime around 1300. They were replaced by other cultures.

One of these cultures is the Ojibwa (sometimes called Chippewa). They lived in present-day Michigan and Ohio. The Ojibwa are part of a group of Native Americans called the Eastern Woodlands peoples. They hunted, fished, and sometimes farmed in the forests and waters of the Midwest before Europeans came to North America. Today there are many Ojibwa reservations in Wisconsin, Michigan, and Minnesota.

The Lakota live in the Midwest, too. They are part of a group known as the Plains peoples. In the past, they lived on the plains of Nebraska, North Dakota, South Dakota, and Minnesota. The Lakota depended on buffalo for food, clothing, and shelter. Today Lakota communities in the Midwest mix modern culture with traditional ways of life.

QUICK CHECK

Summarize **What groups of people lived in the Midwest hundreds of years ago?**

Grave Creek Burial Mound ▶

Early settlers to the Midwest traveled by flatboat.

B PEOPLE OF THE MIDWEST

In the 1500s, European fur traders began exploring the Midwest for a new and inexpensive supply of furs. Around 1770, a fur trader named Jean Baptiste Pointe du Sable began a trading post near Lake Michigan. Du Sable was from the French colony of Haiti, an island in the Caribbean Sea. Du Sable's trading post grew into the city of Chicago.

Heading West

Fur traders shipped their goods to Europe from ports in the Northeast.

Many people in these eastern cities learned about the fertile Midwestern soil. Fertile soil meant a chance for them to make a good living as a farmer. Many decided to move to the Midwest in search of this rich land with endless possibilities.

As more people traveled west, new trails opened. Later settlers traveled along these new trails in covered wagons. These wagons were pulled by horses, mules, or oxen. By 1850, more than five million people had settled in the Midwest.

Most of the Native Americans' land in Ohio, Indiana, and Illinois was taken by soldiers for the new settlers.

These first settlers to travel west were known as **pioneers**. The parents of Abraham Lincoln, our nation's sixteenth president, were pioneers.

New Immigrants

In the late 1800s and early 1900s, the population of the Midwest became more diverse. Norwegian farmers moved to Minnesota and people from Czechoslovakia worked the land in Nebraska. Polish immigrants found factory jobs in Illinois and thousands of Germans and Italians settled in Wisconsin, Missouri, and Ohio.

EVENT

Thousands of African Americans traveled on the **Underground Railroad** to escape slavery in the South. By 1850 nearly 100,000 African Americans had fled to the Midwest and Canada.

Underground Railroad

African Americans in the Midwest

African Americans headed to the Midwest from the South to escape slavery. They traveled on what is now known as the Underground Railroad—a network of people who helped enslaved people escape. William Wells Brown escaped slavery in 1833:

> **❝**As we traveled towards a land of liberty, my heart would at times leap for joy.**❞**

Later, African Americans moved from the South to the Midwest to find jobs and equality. Most settled in factory cities in Illinois, Ohio, and Michigan. Their move north between the years of 1914 and 1950 is called the Great **Migration**. A migration is a journey from one place to another.

QUICK CHECK

Summarize **Describe the different people that have come to the Midwest.**

◄ Midwesterners today come from around the world.

ⓒ THE MIDWEST TODAY

People from across the world continue to move to the Midwest. Many Mexicans have settled in Chicago. Immigrants from East Africa and Southeast Asia live in St. Paul and Minneapolis. Detroit has the largest population of Arab Americans in the United States. Today modern immigrants arrive by car, bus, or plane, not by flatboat or wagon.

Celebrating Cultures and Traditions

Different cultures make the Midwest fun and exciting. Many types of celebrations honor the region's ethnic heritage. People in Holland, Michigan, celebrate their Dutch roots with a tulip festival each spring. Milwaukee, Wisconsin, has a large German festival every summer, and St. Louis, Missouri, holds a Japanese festival every fall.

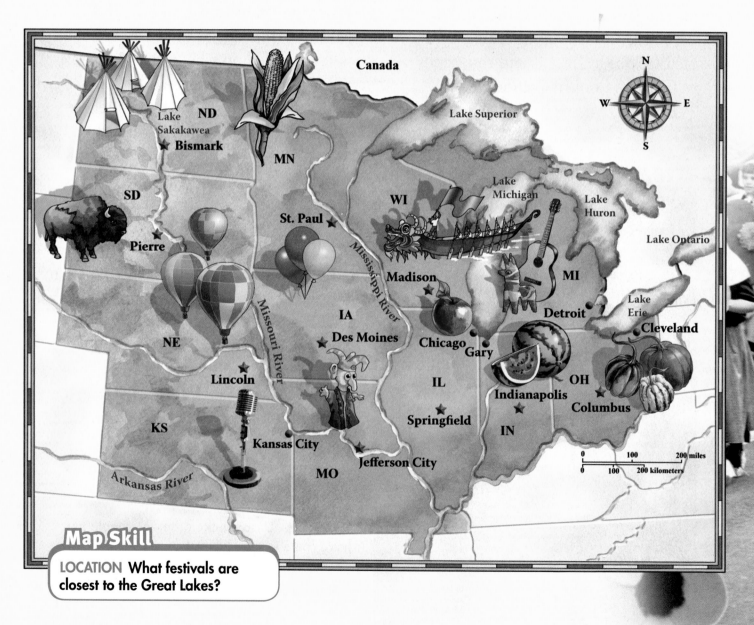

Map Skill

LOCATION **What festivals are closest to the Great Lakes?**

Midwesterners also honor their region's history, weather, and **traditions**, or customs, that make the region a great place to live. St. Paul, Minnesota, holds a Winter Carnival to celebrate the region's cold weather. The Corn Palace in South Dakota is decorated with thousands of cornstalks to celebrate farming. St. Louis is proud of its history as the "Gateway to the West."

Dutch descendants celebrate their heritage during the Tulip Festival in Holland, Michigan. ▼

Legend

🚣 Great Mideast Dragon Boat Festival in Racine, WI

🍎 Apple Festival in Long Grove, IL

🍉 Brownstown Melonfest in Brownstown, IN

🎃 Circleville Pumpkin Show in Circleville, OH

🤹 PuppetFest Midwest in Trenton, MO

🎈 Iowa State Fair in Des Moines, IA

🎸 Tulipanes Latino Art & Film Festival in Holland, MI

🎙 Kansas City Kansas Street Blues Festival

🎈 Hot Air Balloon Festival in Wakefield, NE

🦬 Buffalo Roundup and Arts Festival in Custer State Park, SD

▬ National boundary
State boundary
● Major city
★ State capital

⛺ Northern Plains Indian Culture Fest Stanton, ND

🌽 Hinckley Corn & Clover Festival in Hinckly, MN

Citizenship
Express Your Opinion

Three friends learned that pollution was threatening the brook trout in streams near their township. In an effort to protect the fish, the girls formed a group called Save Our Streams (SOS). They wrote letters and talked with people and leaders in the area to work on a plan for keeping the streams clean.

Write About It Write a letter to your local newspaper expressing your opinion about an issue.

D   MIDWEST ART, MUSIC, AND FUN

Throughout history, the states of the Midwest have been home to many great artists, musicians, writers, and athletes. Some of our nation's best-known writers, for example, are from the Midwest. Laura Ingalls Wilder wrote amazing stories about her life as a pioneer. The poet Thomas Stearns Eliot, known as T. S. Eliot, was born in St. Louis. Read what he had to say about it.

The Midwest is also known for its music. What kinds of music do you like? In the Midwest, the best answer is all of them! Cleveland disc jockey Alan Freed helped develop rock and roll in the 1950s. Today, Cleveland is home to the Rock and Roll Hall of Fame. Detroit is famous for soul music. Kansas City is known for jazz. Bluegrass star Alison Krauss grew up in Illinois.

> I am very well satisfied with having been born in St. Louis.
> —T.S. ELIOT

Sculptor Korczak Ziolkowski moved to South Dakota in 1947 to carve the Crazy Horse monument out of the Black Hills mountains. Although he died in 1982, his children continue working on the monument. ▼

The 500 Mile Race

The largest sport facility in the world is in Indianapolis, Indiana, and is called the Indianapolis Motor Speedway. Every year, it holds the Indy 500 race over Memorial weekend. In 2006, the Indy 500 race celebrated its 90th anniversary. But that's not all that happens at the Speedway. Famous races such as the Allstate 400 and the United States Grand Prix are also held there. These races attract thousands of visitors from around the world.

▲ The Indianapolis 500 is held every year in Indianapolis, Indiana.

QUICK CHECK

Summarize **What are some of the things people in the Midwest do for fun?**

George Clinton and Parliament-Funkadelic perform at the Rock and Roll Hall of Fame. ▼

Check Understanding

1. **VOCABULARY** Use each vocabulary word to describe the people of the Midwest.

   pioneer   **migration**   **tradition**

2. **READING SKILL** Draw Conclusions Use the chart from page 150 to write about why you think the Midwest inspires so many writers and artists.

Text Clues	Conclusion

3. **Write About It** Write a short essay about what the Great Migration might have been like for the people who migrated.

Vocabulary

Copy the sentences below. Use the list of vocabulary words to fill in the blanks.

mass production   iron

fertile   pioneer

1. Wheat and corn are grown in the _____ soil of the Midwest.

2. Henry Ford was one of the first to use _____ in manufacturing.

3. Steel is made in part from a metal known as _____.

4. An early settler of the Midwest is called a _____.

Comprehension and Critical Thinking

5. How were the Great Lakes formed?

6. Who was Jean Baptiste Pointe du Sable?

7. Reading Skill Why is the Midwest home to so many musical styles? Draw conclusions.

8. Critical Thinking What do you think it was like to be a pioneer?

Skill

Use Line and Bar Graphs

Write a complete sentence to answer each question.

9. Which state has the largest population?

10. Which state has the smallest population?

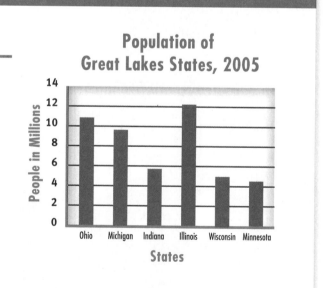

Population of Great Lakes States, 2005

People in Millions — States: Ohio, Michigan, Indiana, Illinois, Wisconsin, Minnesota

 # Illinois Standards Achievement Test Preparation

> Without warm ocean breezes, much of the Midwest is extremely cold in the winter. Icy winds travel across the plains, chilling everything in its path. Sometimes blizzards, or winter storms with strong winds and snow, form. Cities near the Great Lakes receive the heaviest snowfall. This lake effect snow occurs when cold, dry air from Canada meets warmer, damp air over the Great Lakes. Moisture in the air cools and becomes snow. Some areas can receive more than 200 inches of lake effect snow each year.

1 What is one reason that the Midwest is so cold in the winter?

- Ⓐ There are no warm ocean breezes.
- Ⓑ Cold air moves north from the Gulf of Mexico.
- Ⓒ Wet air from Canada makes it cold.
- Ⓓ Winds from the West bring storms to the Midwest.

2 What cities receive the most snowfall?

- Ⓐ Canadian cities
- Ⓑ cities near the Great Lakes
- Ⓒ cities farthest from the Great Lakes
- Ⓓ Midwestern cities do not receive any snowfall because the winters are mild.

3 What happens when dry air from Canada meets warmer, damp air over the Great Lakes?

- Ⓐ temperatures rise
- Ⓑ heavy rainfall
- Ⓒ strong winds blow across the Midwest
- Ⓓ lake effect snow

4 What is a blizzard?

- Ⓐ A spring storm with heavy rainfall.
- Ⓑ A winter storm with strong winds and snow.
- Ⓒ A wind storm that comes from Canada.
- Ⓓ A winter snow storm with more than 200 inches of snow.

How do natural resources affect a region's growth?

Write About the Big Idea

Expository Essay
Use the Unit 5 foldable to help you write an essay that answers the Big Idea question, "How do natural resources affect a region's growth?" Be sure to begin your essay with an introduction. Use the notes you wrote under each tab in the foldable for details to support each main idea. End with a concluding paragraph that answers the question.

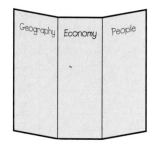

Create a Diorama

Work in a small group to create a diorama showing a pioneer family coming to the Midwest on a flatboat or covered wagon. Here's how you can get started:

1. Research the pioneers who headed west.

2. Choose the structures you would like to represent in your diorama.

3. Choose the materials you will use to build your diorama.

4. Build the pieces and assemble the diorama.

5. Write a paragraph telling what is happening in your diorama.

EXPLORE The Big Idea

Essential Question
What causes a state to change?

FOLDABLES™ Study Organizer

Main Idea and Details
Use the four-tab Foldable as you read this unit. On your tabs, write **People**, **Geography**, **Economy**, and **Government**. Use the Foldable to organize the details in each section.

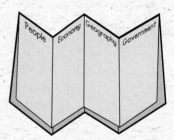

LOG ON

For more about Unit 3 go to www.macmillanmh.com

Abraham Lincoln lived in this house in Springfield, Illinois. It is now a national historic site.

Illinois: The Land of Lincoln

PEOPLE, PLACES, AND EVENTS

Mexican Americans

Mural in Pilsen, Chicago

Pilsen, a Chicago neighborhood, is home to many **Mexican Americans**. This neighborhood is known for its beautiful **murals**. The murals represent Mexican history and culture, and the concerns of the Mexican community.

Today, you can go to Pilsen to see the many colorful murals decorating the walls of buildings in this neighborhood.

Jin Lee

Photo of Prairie by Jin Lee

The artist **Jin Lee** has produced many works of art focusing on **prairies**. Some of her work is in the permanent collection at the Art Institute of Chicago.

Today, you can visit the Midewin National Tallgrass Prairie near Elwood, Illinois. In 1996 the United States government made the MNTP a preserved, or protected, prairie.

Summer Interns

Aon Center in Chicago, IL

Each summer, the Chicago World Trade Center, which includes the **Aon Center,** offers a program to college students. Students interested in international business can get professional experience working as **summer interns**.

Today, you can travel to the Aon Center in Chicago. It is the third-tallest building in the United States.

Old State Capitol in Springfield

**Governor
Rod R. Blagojevich**

Current Illinois governor, **Rod R. Blagojevich**, works in the Illinois State Capitol in Springfield. This building replaced the old Capitol building as home of the Illinois government in 1876.

Today, you can tour the **Old State Capitol** building, where Abraham Lincoln spent much of his time. It was the fifth capitol in Illinois history, but the first capitol in Springfield.

One State, Many People

Lesson 1

VOCABULARY

ancestor p. 165

traditional p. 167

veteran p. 168

READING SKILL

Main Idea and Details
Copy the chart below. As you read, fill it in with the main idea and details about the people of Illinois.

Main Idea	Details

Illinois Learning Standards

16.D.2(W), 18.A.2, 18.B.2a, 18.C.2

The Chicago White Sox play baseball at U.S. Cellular Field.

Visual Preview

How do the people of Illinois shape the state?

A Illinoisans come from all parts of the world and bring their cultures with them.

B Illinoisans celebrate their cultures and the people of their state.

C Illinoisans care about their communities and their veterans.

Ⓐ THE PEOPLE OF ILLINOIS

Almost 13 million people live in our state. Some live in large cities. Some live in small cities or on farms. What are we like? Where did we come from? What do we celebrate?

People arrive in Illinois from all parts of the world. Our **ancestors**, or relatives from the past, were immigrants who came from many different countries.

A Diverse State

Many of us trace our roots back to countries in Europe, such as Germany, Sweden, Poland, and Ireland. Some people come to Illinois from countries in Asia and Latin America. Asian Americans make up about 4 percent of our population, while Hispanic Americans make up about 14 percent.

The Chicago neighborhood of Pilsen attracts immigrants from Mexico. Pilsen is known for its colorful murals. The murals show pride in Mexican heritage. Chinatown is home to about 70,000 Chinese Americans. A colorful gate marks the entrance to this neighborhood.

African Americans make up about 15 percent of the Illinois population. Many have ancestors who came from southern states after the Civil War.

More moved to Illinois cities such as Chicago, Aurora, and Peoria after World War I.

When people moved to Illinois, they brought their cultures with them. Culture includes a people's history, language, religion, and customs.

QUICK CHECK

Main Idea and Details What are four groups important to Illinois's population today?

▲ Dancers at the Autumn Moon Festival in Chicago's Chinatown

LINCOLN'S BIRTHDAY

SWEDISH DAY

B CELEBRATIONS AND FESTIVALS

The combination of cultures in Illinois has helped to shape the state. Today, there are many holidays and festivals in Illinois. They celebrate different cultures.

Honoring Historical Figures

Abraham Lincoln, our nation's sixteenth President, lived in Illinois for most of his life. His Presidential Library and Museum is located in Springfield. To mark Lincoln's birthday, in February the museum plans a day full of festivities. Speakers talk about Lincoln's life. There are also crafts, party games, and music.

Have you heard of Pulaski Day? It is an official Illinois state holiday. It honors Kazimierz Pulaski, a Polish hero of the American Revolution. He served under George Washington. Pulaski Day falls on the first Monday in March. Many Illinois schools and businesses close for the day.

Celebrating Our Cultures

Four days in July, the streets of Pilsen are filled with the sounds and smells of Mexican music and food. It is Fiesta del Sol! Tourists from around the world visit just for this cultural event.

FIESTA DEL SOL

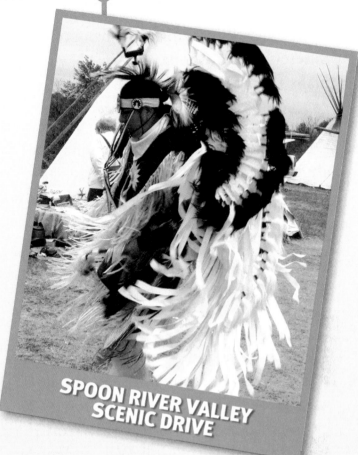

SPOON RIVER VALLEY SCENIC DRIVE

The city of Geneva hosts Swedish Days each June. It is a six-day celebration of our ancestors from Sweden. People enjoy music, dances, and a parade. They also eat **traditional** foods, like Swedish meatballs and Swedish pancakes. Traditional means something that comes from the past.

Each October, Fulton County has a fall festival. It is called the Spoon River Valley Scenic Drive. During the Drive, towns throughout the county hold celebrations of history and culture. Mount Pisgah celebrates with Native American dancers. The Dickson Mounds Museum in Lewistown re-creates life in Illinois in the 1700s. People dressed as English and

French colonists teach early American crafts and skills. Thousands of people come to take part in this festival.

QUICK CHECK

Main Idea and Details **How do people celebrate their cultures?**

PEOPLE

Our nation's sixteenth president, Abraham Lincoln, lived in Springfield for much of his life. He was the president during the Civil War.

Abraham Lincoln

167

Although Illinoisans come from many different backgrounds, they still have many things in common.

Caring for Others

Like other Americans, Illinoisans care about community. Camp Callahan is a summer camp for mentally and physically challenged children and adults in Adams County. Camp Callahan has been open for more than 50 years. Thanks to community volunteers, the camp is free.

A Sense of Pride

Illinoisans also share pride in honoring **veterans**. A veteran is a man or woman who has served in the military. Illinoisans have served in the War of 1812, World War II, the Persian Gulf War, and more.

▼ Illinoisans honor war veterans in a Memorial Day ceremony in Jacksonville, Illinois

To honor our veterans, many Illinois towns and cities have built memorials. A memorial is something that serves as a remembrance of a person or event. The people of Mt. Vernon helped raise money to create a memorial that now stands in Mt. Vernon's Veterans' Park. Illinoisans also honor veterans by celebrating Veteran's Day, a national holiday in November.

QUICK CHECK

Main Idea and Details **What two qualities do Illinoisans have in common with other Americans?**

Check Understanding

1. **VOCABULARY** Write a sentence for each vocabulary word.
   ancestor   traditional   veteran

2. **READING SKILL Main Idea and Details** Use your chart from page 164 to describe one Illinois festival or celebration.

Main Idea	Details

 3. **Write About It** How did groups of immigrants change Illinois over time?

Chart and Graph Skills

Read Circle Graphs

VOCABULARY
circle graph

A graph is a drawing that helps you compare information by displaying the relationship between things. The graph below is a **circle graph**. Circle graphs show how parts of something fit into the whole. Because each part looks like a slice of pie, a circle graph is sometimes called a pie graph.

Learn It

- The title of the graph tells you what is displayed in the graph. This circle graph shows the U.S. states that produce the most corn.

- The labels tell you what each slice represents. You can see that the red slice stands for the percentage of corn that is grown in Illinois.

- A larger slice means more corn is grown in that state.

Leading U.S. States in the Production of Corn

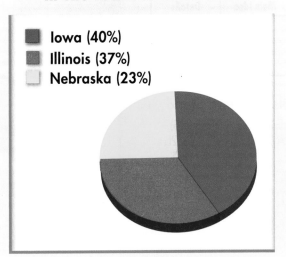

- Iowa (40%)
- Illinois (37%)
- Nebraska (23%)

Try It

- Compare the slices. Which state grows the most corn?

- Which state grows more corn, Nebraska or Illinois?

- Which state grows the least amount of corn?

Apply It

- Make a circle graph showing how much time you spend doing each of the following activities during one school day: sleep, eat, learn, watch TV, play sports, and do homework. Feel free to add any other activities that you do.

B LAND AND WATER

Suppose you could fly over Illinois and look below. What would you see?

The Central Plains

The Central Plains region of Illinois covers about 90 percent of the state. This region has rolling hills and prairies. Prairies are flat or rolling land with few trees. Hills and prairies are both **landforms**, or natural features on Earth's surface.

Landforms in the Central Plains are a result of glaciers. Long ago, much of Illinois was covered in glaciers. The glaciers moved slowly across the land, carrying soil and rocks. In many areas, glaciers filled valleys and flattened hills, creating prairies. In other areas, they carved out streams and rivers.

The glaciers left behind rich soil, Illinois's greatest natural resource. Crops grow well in this rich soil. Farms growing corn, soybeans, and other grains cover much of the Central Plains today. Farms in Illinois grow more corn than almost any other state.

The Shawnee Hills

South of the Central Plains, you can find rivers, valleys, and forests. This is the Shawnee Hills region. Glaciers never covered this land, so it is rougher and hillier than the Central Plains. Much of the Shawnee Hills is rich in natural resources, including coal and fluorite. Fluorite can be used to process steel. Petroleum is another important resource. Illinois produces more petroleum than most Midwestern states.

The Shawnee Hills were never covered by glaciers.

The Gulf Coastal Plain

The extreme southern tip of Illinois is covered by part of the Gulf Coastal Plain. The plain stretches north from the Gulf of Mexico. South of the Shawnee Hills, the plain tends to be hilly, but it flattens toward the Illinois border with Kentucky.

Lakes, Rivers, and Streams

Our state has about 900 streams. Three-fourths of them empty into the Mississippi River. This great river winds its way south through the Midwest and empties into the Gulf of Mexico.

Illinois also has many lakes. Most of these lakes were made by humans. Rend Lake is one example. Engineers built a dam across the Big Muddy River. Water backed up behind the dam to form Rend Lake. It supplies water to about 300,000 people each day. It is also used for recreation. Visitors like to fish, swim, boat, and camp at Rend Lake.

Illinois is bordered by Lake Michigan, which is the largest freshwater lake in the United States. Lake Michigan is one of the Great Lakes, formed long ago by melting glaciers. The beaches of its southern shoreline are covered in soft sand. Chicago, located on Lake Michigan, has 29 lakefront beaches.

QUICK CHECK

Main Idea and Details **What are three land regions in Illinois?**

The West Chicago Prairie Forest Preserve protects prairie land, along with its many plants and wildlife. ▼

Did you know that the climate in the northern parts of Illinois is different from the climate in its southern parts? Usually the southern part of the state is warmer than the northern part.

The Lake Effect

Southern Illinois typically gets 14 inches of snow each year. Chicago receives three times that amount because it experiences lake effect snow. The snow occurs after winds travel over a large lake, like Lake Michigan. The wind picks up water vapor. When the wind reaches colder land, the vapor turns to snow.

Winter storms in Illinois can be very damaging. Between November and April, they bring freezing winds and dangerous ice. Each year, Illinois experiences many of these fierce storms.

Terrible Winds

Tornadoes are another form of severe weather that occurs in Illinois. A tornado is a fast-moving column of air which looks like a funnel. The funnel typically extends from a thunderstorm and makes contact with the ground. Often a cloud of debris encircles the lower portion of the funnel.

During the winter months children go sledding.

Illinois Annual Snowfall

(Bar graph showing Inches of Snow for Illinois Cities: Chicago ~38, Springfield ~26, Peoria ~26, Cairo ~11, Quincy ~22, Glenview ~45)

Chart Skill

LOCATION Which two Illinois cities on the graph have the smallest yearly snowfall?

EVENT

Two of the worst tornadoes in United States history hit Illinois. On March 18, 1925, the **Tri-State tornado** killed nearly 700 people. The **Mattoon tornado** on May 26, 1917, killed about 100 people. Both tornadoes caused incredible damage.

Tornado Damage

An average of 28 tornadoes strike Illinois each year.

The strongest tornadoes spin at speeds greater than 200 miles per hour. They can leave a path of destruction 50 miles long and a mile wide. This is how one person describes a tornado:

> ❝It was just a loud constant rumbling. You could hear the wind being sucked into the tornado.❞

Climate Extremes

Illinois can get extremely hot in the summer and extremely cold in the winter. East St. Louis holds the record for the highest temperature in the state, at 117°F. Congerville holds the record for the lowest temperature in the state, at -36°F.

QUICK CHECK

Main Idea and Details **What are tornadoes?**

Check Understanding

1. **VOCABULARY** Draw a picture for each word and label each picture.
   border   landform

2. **READING SKILL** Main Idea and Details Use your chart from page 170 to write about the climate of Illinois.

Main Idea	Details

3. **Write About It** Describe how glaciers shaped the land in Illinois.

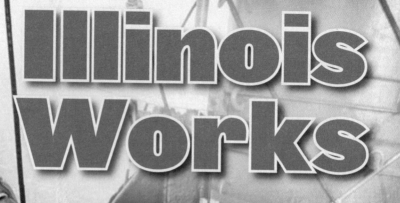

Illinois Works

VOCABULARY

service p. 177

manufacturing p. 178

trade p. 179

export p. 179

READING SKILL

Main Idea and Details
Copy the chart below.
As you read, fill it in with
the main idea and details
about jobs in Illinois.

Main Idea	Details

Illinois Learning Standards
15.A.2a, 15.A.2b, 15.D.2a

Service worker fixing an antenna on top of the
John Hancock building in Chicago, Illinois

Visual Preview

How have Illinois jobs changed over time?

A The main industry in Illinois changed from agriculture to service.

B Products made in Illinois are sold around the world.

C Farmers and miners find new ways to use our state's natural resources.

176

A   SERVICE INDUSTRIES

There are many different types of jobs in Illinois. You can do work for others, make or design your own products, or work with the state's natural resources. What kind of job would you like?

Illinois has many industries that make up its economy. In the 1870s, agriculture, or farming, was the state's main industry. Today, Illinois's largest economic industries are business, finance, and **services.**

Service Jobs

Service is work done for someone else. In a restaurant, the host, server, and cook all do work for their customers. They are service workers. Firefighters, doctors, and lawyers are service workers, too. Can you name other service jobs?

Look around your classroom. Your teacher works in the service industry.

Value of Education

Whatever career you choose, the amount of education you have is valuable. Your income is often directly related to your education and experience. For example, doctors may earn more money than cooks because they have more years of education.

QUICK CHECK

Main Idea and Details **What are examples of service industry jobs?**

Percentage of Illinois Workers in Various Industries	
Service	🧍🧍🧍🧍 ˮ
Agriculture and Mining	🧍 ᵀ
Manufacturing and Construction	🧍

🧍 = 1 million workers

Chart Skill

In which industry do the least number of Illinoisians work?

Firefighters work in the service industry. ▶

Although agriculture is no longer the leading industry in Illinois, it still plays an important role in the state's economy.

A Farmer's Life

In Lesson 2, you learned that our state's greatest natural resource is our soil. Farmers use the rich, black soil to grow many different crops. Illinois has about 76,000 farms. Most are family-owned. They cover nearly 80 percent of the state's land.

Illinois is the country's second largest producer of corn and soybeans. Our farmers also grow wheat, barley, oats, and hay. They raise dairy cows, pigs, sheep, and turkeys. Illinois also grows large amounts of flowers to sell, like roses and carnations.

At a farmer's market, you can get fresh fruits and vegetables grown by local farmers. ▼

DataGraphic

Facts About Illinois Farms

Illinois farms grow many different crops, including a large amount of corn and soybeans.

Agricultural Products

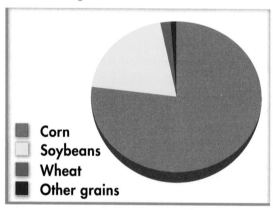

- Corn
- Soybeans
- Wheat
- Other grains

Distibution of Major Crops

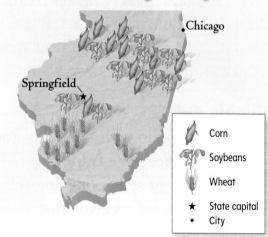

Chicago

Springfield

- Corn
- Soybeans
- Wheat
- ★ State capital
- • City

Think About Agriculture

1. Which is the major crop in Illinios?

2. In what part of the state is corn grown mostly?

Limestone is dug from quarries in Illinois. ▲

Technology and Farming

New technologies have helped improve soil, water, and nutrients that farmers use. They have also helped remove pests. Education is important in creating and improving these new technologies. Many farmers study new technologies to learn about better farming methods.

Digging for Minerals

Many of the great natural resources in Illinois are hidden underground. Minerals such as coal and limestone are found in all parts of the state.

Coal-fired power plants make the electricity that powers televisions and lights in our homes. About one-eighth of all the coal in the United States is found in Illinois.

Limestone is one of the state's most valuable resources. It is used to make road surfaces and to improve soil for farming.

QUICK CHECK

Main Idea and Details **What are two ways that limestone is used?**

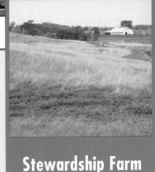

PLACES

Located in Piatt County, the **Stewardship Farm** is a farm that helps protect natural resources and improve natural farming methods.

Stewardship Farm

Check Understanding

1. **VOCABULARY** Use both of the words below in a paragraph about jobs in Illinois.

   service   manufacturing

   trade   export

2. **READING SKILL** Main Idea and Details Use your chart from page 176 to write a sentence describing mining in Illinois.

Main Idea	Details

3. **Write About It** Write about the ways our state might change if we had fewer farms.

Lesson 4

VOCABULARY

ballot p. 184

appeal p. 185

ordinance p. 187

READING SKILL

Main Idea and Details
Copy the chart below. As you read, fill it in with the main idea and details about the government of Illinois.

Main Idea	Details

Illinois Learning Standards
14.A.2, 14.B.2, 14.C.2, 14.D.2.

ILLINOIS'S GOVERNMENT

A statue of Abraham Lincoln welcomes visitors to the Illinois State Capitol building in Springfield, Illinois.

Visual Preview

How is Illinois governed?

A Our government is based on the Illinois constitution.

B The people elect the members of the three branches of state government.

C Local government provides many services.

D You can make a difference in our government.

ILLINOIS CONSTITUTION

What do citizens of Chicago and Quincy have in common?
They are all affected by the actions of the Illinois government.
The Illinois government works to help the citizens of Illinois.

The government of our state is modeled after the government of our country, the United States of America. Just as the United States has a Constitution, so does the state of Illinois. The Illinois Constitution was adopted on December 3, 1818, when Illinois officially became a state.

Why a Constitution?

The Illinois Constitution explains the branches of government. It also explains the powers and responsibilities of our governmen and our rights as citizens.

So far, Illinois has had four different constitutions. Why so many? Life today is very different from life in 1818. As the needs of Illinoisans changed, adjustments were made to the Constitution to meet those needs. The most recent Illlinois Constitution was adopted in 1970.

QUICK CHECK

Main Idea and Details In what year did Illinois officially become a state?

Primary Sources

"All men are by nature free and independent and have certain inherent and inalienable rights among which are life, liberty and the pursuit of happiness. To secure these rights and the protection of property, governments are instituted among men, deriving their just powers from the consent of the governed."

A Section of the Bill of Rights from the Illinois Constitution

Write About It Read this selection from the Illinois Constitution. Write what you think it means.

THREE BRANCHES OF THE ILLINOIS GOVERNMENT

SEAL OF THE STATE OF ILLINOIS

UNION
NATIONAL
SOVEREIGNTY
STATE
1868
1818
AUG. 26TH 1818

EXECUTIVE BRANCH

GOVERNOR
- **Carries out laws**
- **Plans Illinois's budget**

B   THREE BRANCHES OF GOVERNMENT

Like our national government, the Illinois government is divided into three branches.

The Legislative Branch

The legislative branch makes laws. The group of elected men and women who make and pass these laws is the legislature. Illinois's legislature is called the General Assembly. It has two branches—the House of Representatives and the Senate. The House of Representatives has 118 members. The Senate has 59 members.

The Executive Branch

The executive branch carries out the laws. The governor is the head of the executive branch. He has the power to approve new laws. Illinois's governor is Rod R. Blagojevich. He works in the State Capitol Building in Springfield.

Every four years, voters cast **ballots** to decide who will be the governor of Illinois. A ballot is the act or method of voting. It can be cast on paper or on machines. A person can be governor for as long as voters keep electing him or her.

LEGISLATIVE BRANCH

GENERAL ASSEMBLY

- 59 Senators
- 118 Representatives
- Makes laws for the state

JUDICIAL BRANCH

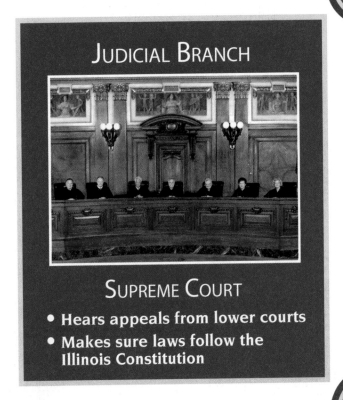

SUPREME COURT

- Hears appeals from lower courts
- Makes sure laws follow the Illinois Constitution

The five other members of Illinois's executive branch are the lieutenant governor, attorney general, secretary of state, comptroller, and treasurer. The executive branch is elected by voters.

The Judicial Branch

The judicial branch is made up of the Supreme Court, the Appellate Court, and the Circuit Court. The Supreme Court is the highest court in the state of Illinois. Seven judges serve on it. They are elected from the five judicial districts in the state. The district that includes Cook County is represented by three justices. The other four districts have one each. Each justice is elected for a term of 10 years.

The chief justice is elected by the court from its members for a 3-year term. The Supreme Court has authority over all courts in the state.

Supreme Court judges perform many tasks. They interpret our state's Constitution. They decide if the laws passed by the legislature follow the Constitution. One of the most important responsibilities of the Supreme Court is to hear **appeals** from lower courts. An appeal is a request to review a case that has already been tried.

QUICK CHECK

Main Idea and Details **What are the three branches of the state government of Illinois?**

▲ Barack Obama, one of two Illinois senators, answers questions in a town hall meeting.

Some Departments of Local Government

FIRE DEPARTMENT
provides ambulance, fire, and rescue services

PARKS AND RECREATION DEPARTMENT
maintains parks

PLANNING DEPARTMENT
plans for city projects

POLICE DEPARTMENT
keeps citizens safe

PUBLIC HEALTH DEPARTMENT
helps citizens fight disease

BUILDING INSPECTION DEPARTMENT
grants permits for new buildings, inspects plans

ENVIRONMENTAL SERVICES DEPARTMENT
oversees garbage, recycling

FINANCE DEPARTMENT
collects taxes, handles city money

MAINTENANCE DEPARTMENT
repairs streets, signs, traffic lights

Can you imagine life without schools, hospitals, libraries, parks, or garbage removal? All of these services, and many more, are provided by local government.

Three Levels of Local Government

The local government system of Illinois has almost 7,000 parts. There are three basic levels. They are county, township, and municipality.

The top level of local government is the county. Voters in each county elect officials. These officials include board members, circuit court clerks, sheriffs, and school superintendents.

The middle level of local government is the township. Voters in townships elect judges and local officials, such as the town clerk. Most Illinois townships hold annual town meetings for all township voters. People come to the meetings to discuss and debate important issues.

The most local unit of local government is the municipality. A municipality is a city, village, or town. Let us focus on one Illinois municipality, the city of Darien.

One Town's Government

Darien is a municipality located west of Chicago. The municipality is run by a mayor, council members, and an official called an administrator.

Darien's mayor is the head of the municipality's government. The mayor leads the council. Similar to the governor, the mayor enforces local laws.

The council in Darien adopts local **ordinances**. An ordinance is a law. A municipality's council can be compared to the state's legislature. The council also manages the municipality's money.

The administrator manages the municipality's employees. He or she also carries out the plans and projects approved by the mayor and council.

QUICK CHECK

Main Idea and Details **What are the three basic levels of local government in Illinois?**

Citizenship

Leadership/Justice

Some laws start out as ideas from citizens. When the idea of a bill, or an idea for a law is developed, the text must be written. Then, a member of Congress must officially introduce the bill in Congress. Representatives usually sponsor bills that are important to them and their citizens.

In 1974, a class of Illinois schoolchildren proposed a bill. They wanted to make the monarch butterfly the official insect of Illinois. Their state representative introduced the bill, and in 1975 it was signed into a law.

Write About It Think of a new law that would help the people of Illinois. Write a paragraph describing your law. Explain why it is important.

Vocabulary

Number a paper from 1 to 4. Beside each number, write the word from the list that matches the description.

landform   export

trade   ballot

1. A natural feature on the Earth's surface is a _____.

2. Voters cast a _____.

3. _____ means to buy or sell goods.

4. _____ means to send goods to other countries.

Comprehension and Critical Thinking

5. Describe the population of Illinois.

6. In what type of industry do most Illinoisans work?

7. **Reading Skill** Why is it important for Illinois to trade with other countries?

8. **Critical Thinking** Compare and contrast two branches of Illinois's government.

Skill

Use Road Maps

Write a complete sentence to answer each question.

9. In which direction does state highway 51 run?

10. Which roads would you take to travel from Springfield to Peoria?

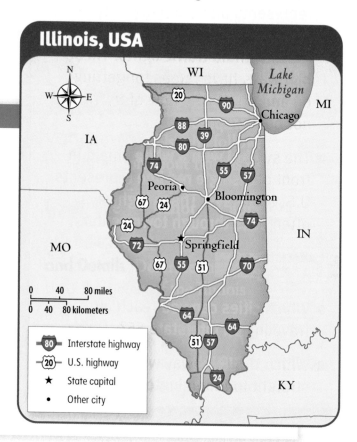

Illinois, USA

Illinois Standards Achievement Test Preparation

John Deere

John Deere developed the first plow. The plow was very successful and John Deere and his partner sold a lot of them. By 1855 he was selling more than 13,000 plows a year.

John Deere was born in Rutland, Vermont. He was an apprentice to a blacksmith. He moved to Grand Detour, Illinois in 1837. In 1868 his business was incorporated as Deere & Company. The company is still very successful.

1

Whose job did John Deere's invention improve?

Ⓐ butchers
Ⓑ farmers
Ⓒ miners
Ⓓ truck drivers

2

Paragraph 2 of this biography is mainly about —

Ⓐ John Deere's partner
Ⓑ the Illinois prairies
Ⓒ John Deere's personal background
Ⓓ the future of Deere & Company

3

When did Deere incorporate his company?

Ⓐ 1837
Ⓑ 1855
Ⓒ 1886
Ⓓ 1868

4

Which of these is a true statement about John Deere?

Ⓐ He created a successful company.
Ⓑ He struggled to succeed.
Ⓒ He was born and raised in Illinois.
Ⓓ He was a farmer.

The Big Idea Review

What causes a state to change?

Write About the Big Idea

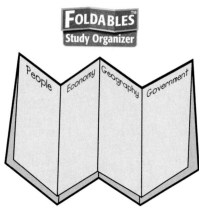

FOLDABLES™
Study Organizer

Expository Essay
Use your Unit 4 Foldable to help you write an expository essay. Answer the Big Idea question—What causes a state to change? Be sure to begin with a sentence that tells the topic of the composition. Include one paragraph for each detail on your Foldable. End with a concluding paragraph that summarizes your composition.

Make a Holiday Poster

With a partner, create a poster showing how a holiday or festival is celebrated in your community. Here are steps to get you started.

1. Research the holidays and festivals that are celebrated in your community, and choose one of them.

2. Get poster board.

3. Use markers or crayons to illustrate how you celebrate that holiday or festival.

4. Add a short explanation about what you drew and present it to the class.

Lincoln's Birthday

The Life of Abraham Lincoln

We celebrate Lincoln's Birthday by dressing up as Abraham Lincoln, reading books about his life, and baking a BIG Lincoln cake!

The Story of Illinois

Unit 5

EXPLORE The Big Idea

Essential Question
How do people and events shape the history and culture of a state?

FOLDABLES Study Organizer

Summarize
Use a three-tab book Foldable to take notes as you read Unit 5.

Label the three tabs **First People of Illinois, A Growing State,** and **Illinois Today**.

LOG ON

For more about Unit 2 go to
www.macmillanmh.com

An ear of corn and a beaker of ethanol produced at the Adkins Energy Ethanol Production Facility near Lena, Illinois.

500 mL
PYREX®
Made in Germany

5100
STOPPER No. 10

193

PEOPLE, PLACES, AND EVENTS

Cyrus McCormick

The Reaper

Cyrus McCormick made farming easier by inventing the **reaper**—a machine that cut wheat and other crops. Before the reaper, farmers had to cut crops by hand.

Today, you can visit the **Southwestern Farm and Home Museum** in Shipman, Illinois, to see an original reaper and other early farm machinery.

Barge on I&M Canal

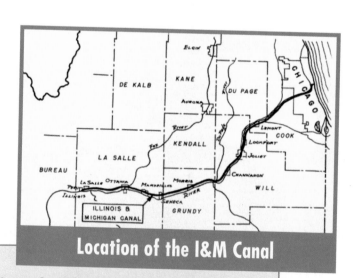
Location of the I&M Canal

The building of the **Illinois and Michigan Canal** in 1848 linked Lake Michigan and the Illinois River. This created a water passage from the Great Lakes to the Gulf of Mexico.

Today, you can follow the route of the I&M Canal by walking or biking the Illinois and Michigan Canal State Trail.

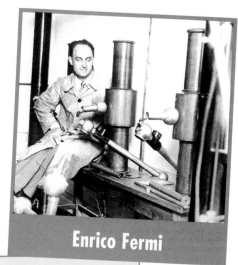

Enrico Fermi

First Controlled Nuclear Chain Reaction

In 1942 **Enrico Fermi** and a team of scientists set off the world's first controlled **nuclear chain reaction**. This led to a new age in science, called the atomic age.

Today, you can see a sculpture and plaque honoring Fermi's experiment. They are located at the University of Chicago, on the site where the experiment took place.

Pritzer Pavilion

Millenium Park

Millenium Park is located in the heart of downtown Chicago. Aside from beautiful landscapes, this huge park has sculptures, fountains, outdoor theaters, and an ice rink.

Today, you can visit Millenium Park to splash around in the Crown Fountain and to attend the **Grant Park Music Festival** in the Pritzer Pavilion.

Becoming a State

VOCABULARY

Illiniwek p. 197

Cahokia p. 199

debate p. 202

READING SKILL

Summarize

Copy the chart below. As you read, fill it in with a summary of the events that changed Illinois.

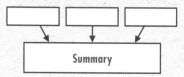

Summary

Illinois Learning Standards

16.A.2b, 16.B.2a(W), 16.B.2d(US)

Frenchman Robert La Salle and his group feasting in an Illiniwek village in 1680

Visual Preview

How did people change the area we call Illinois today?

A The Illiniwek lived in villages in the area and gave the state its name.

B French settlers traded fur, built missions, and lost the area to the British.

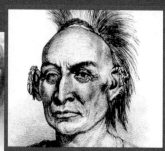

C Settlers pushed for statehood and drove out Native Americans.

D Illinoisans fought for the Union during the Civil War.

Ⓐ THE FIRST PEOPLE OF ILLINOIS

Native Americans have lived in present-day Illinois for more than 12,000 years. One group who lived there when the European settlers arrived 400 years ago gave the state its name.

As you learned in Unit 2, some of the earliest people in the Midwest were the Mississippians. Another group who settled in present-day Illinois were called the **Illiniwek**—or Illini. When French settlers came to the area, they pronounced the name "Illinois," and the name stuck. Look at the chart below to compare the Mississippians and the Illiniwek.

The Illiniwek controlled the area until the end of the 1600s, when Europeans and a Native American group, the Iroquois, arrived.

QUICK CHECK

Summarize **How did Illinois get its name?**

THE ILLINIWEK

- Lived in villages in the 1600s
- Built longhouses for up to ten families and built wigwams near winter camps
- Hunted bison, bear, elk, turkey, and deer on foot with bows and arrows
- Fished the rivers using spears
- Chipped at stones to make spear tips and knives to use and trade
- Women spun bison hair into yarn, wove cloth and reed mats, and made pots with clay
- Women gathered wild nuts and berries; planted maize, beans, squash, and pumpkins

THE MISSISSIPPIANS

- Lived along the Mississippi River from A.D. 700 to 1450
- Built earth mounds for their leaders to live on
- Protected cities with tall log fences, or stockades
- Made pottery, stone tools, and masks
- Traded corn, tools, and beads with other native peoples
- Fought with other native peoples

B THE FRENCH AND ENGLISH

French settlers came from Europe to North America in the 1600s. They settled in an area called New France. Once they settled the governor wanted to find a river route through the continent.

Explorers Jolliet, Marquette, and La Salle

The governor sent two explorers to find the river route. He sent fur trapper Louis Jolliet and priest Jacques Marquette. In 1673 the two left with a group of five men to find the route. They traveled in canoes along Lake Michigan and the Mississippi and Illinois Rivers.

▼ La Salle and his team traveled along the Mississippi River.

As they explored, they met the Illiniwek people. Over a period of 25 years French explorers built several settlements in the area of present-day Illinois.

In 1680 Frenchman Robert La Salle built a fort near the city of Peoria. In 1699 he and other priests established the first permanent settlement in the Illinois region at **Cahokia**. Four years later Jesuit priests founded Kaskaskia. The fur trade and life centered around these towns.

▲ General George Rogers Clark

War and Revolution

By the 1700s, the French controlled much of central North America. But British settlers in the east were pushing west. They battled with the French and Native Americans in the Ohio River Valley. For seven years they fought the French and Indian War. Finally, in 1763, a peace treaty ordered that "Illinois Country" be turned over to the British.

The Revolutionary War began 13 years later. A Virginian general named George Rogers Clark found out that the British wanted Native Americans to fight against American settlers in Illinois. Clark and his troops took control of forts.

QUICK CHECK

Summarize How did French and British explorers change life in Illinois?

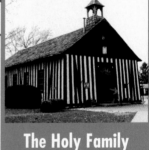

PLACES

Rebuilt in 1799, this church in Cahokia, Illinois has served people since it was first built as a mission in 1699. The church is still used today.

The Holy Family Church

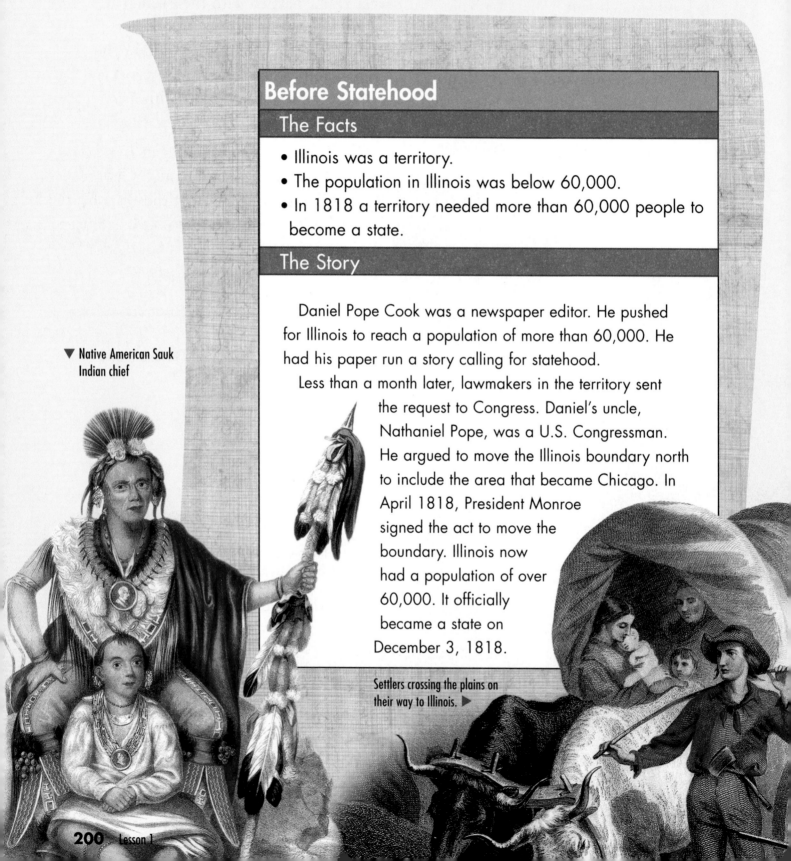

ⓒ THE TWENTY-FIRST STATE

An editor and his uncle, a U.S. Congressman, pushed for statehood. Illinois became a state on December 3, 1818.

Before Statehood

The Facts

- Illinois was a territory.
- The population in Illinois was below 60,000.
- In 1818 a territory needed more than 60,000 people to become a state.

The Story

Daniel Pope Cook was a newspaper editor. He pushed for Illinois to reach a population of more than 60,000. He had his paper run a story calling for statehood.

Less than a month later, lawmakers in the territory sent the request to Congress. Daniel's uncle, Nathaniel Pope, was a U.S. Congressman. He argued to move the Illinois boundary north to include the area that became Chicago. In April 1818, President Monroe signed the act to move the boundary. Illinois now had a population of over 60,000. It officially became a state on December 3, 1818.

▼ Native American Sauk Indian chief

Settlers crossing the plains on their way to Illinois. ▶

After Statehood

The Facts

- Illinois's white population grew to 150,000 by 1830.
- Native Americans in Illinois were forced to sign more than 28 treaties that took away their land.
- Only about 8,000 Native Americans were left in the state.
- In the early and mid-1800s, newcomers from the eastern United States and Europe flooded into northern Illinois.

The Story

As the white population of Illinois grew, Native Americans were made to sign treaties and move west across the Mississippi River. Black Hawk, a leader of a group of Fox and Sauk, refused to accept the treaties. The U.S. government had already taken more than 26 million acres of land.

Black Hawk rebelled and brought 400 families back to Illinois after hunting season. In 1832 battles broke out between his people and U.S. troops. Black Hawk tried to hold his ground but was defeated at the Bad Axe River.

With the Native Americans driven out of Illinois, a land rush began. Many of the new immigrants came along the Erie Canal. Some came to Chicago to build another great water route—the Illinois and Michigan Canal.

QUICK CHECK

Summarize **How did the population of Illinois change after statehood?**

▲ Black Hawk

▼ Settlers traveling to Illinois on a grain boat on the Erie Canal

D THE CIVIL WAR

Illinois was not the scene of famous battles during the Civil War, but some important events did take place here.

A Free State?

Illinois joined the Union as a free state. This meant that slavery was not allowed. Yet state laws kept African Americans from owning land or voting. In the years after statehood, the African American population grew tremendously. By 1848 Illinois had changed its constitution to prevent free African Americans from coming into the state.

Debating Slavery

Most southern Illinois counties favored slavery, while the northern counties did not.

▲ Envelope showing the Illinois state seal.

In 1858 Stephen Douglas and Abraham Lincoln ran for a seat in the U.S. Senate. They held **debates**, or formal arguments and speeches, in seven Illinois towns. Lincoln believed slavery should not be allowed in any new state or territory. Douglas believed that the people living in each area should decide.

In the end, Douglas won the election. But Lincoln swayed the minds of many people. He said the Declaration of Independence gave all people the same natural rights. Lincoln won the U.S. presidency in 1860 and became president in 1861.

▼ Lincoln–Douglas debates, 1858

North Against South

By 1861 the whole nation was fighting over the issue of slavery. President Lincoln called on the nation to send troops to fight for the Union in the Civil War. Illinois responded. More than 250,000 men from Illinois joined the Union army. Stephen Douglas donated land near Chicago for a soldiers' training base. It was called Camp Douglas.

The state also had many major supply bases during the war. A large one was located in Cairo, where the Mississippi and Ohio Rivers meet.

▲ Camp Douglas held prisoners of war from the South later in the war.

QUICK CHECK

Summarize **What major effect did Illinois have on politics in the 1860s?**

A house divided against itself cannot stand. I believe this government cannot endure permanently half-slave and half-free.

—ABRAHAM LINCOLN

Check Understanding

1. **VOCABULARY** Write a sentence for each of the words below.

   Illiniwek   **Cahokia**   **debate**

2. **READING SKILL Summarize**
   Use the chart from page 196 to explain how statehood brought change to the people of Illinois.

3. **Write About It** What effect did the Civil War have on Illinois?

VOCABULARY

Gilded Age p. 206

reform p. 206

settlement house p. 207

exposition p. 209

READING SKILL

Summarize

Copy the chart below. As you read, fill it in with the challenges Illinois faced.

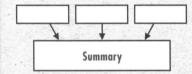

Summary

Illinois Learning Standards

16.A.2b, 16.C.2b(US), 16.C. 2c(US), 16.D.2(W)

Challenges of a Growing State

A bustling Chicago street, 1903

Visual Preview

How did people deal with challenges to the state?

A Chicago was rebuilt after a great fire.

B Labor unions pushed for reform laws for workers.

C Illinois was home to many inventions and the World's Columbian Exposition.

THE GREAT CHICAGO FIRE

What do a lantern, a skyscraper, and a Ferris wheel have to do with one another? They brought great change to the city of Chicago.

After the Civil War, Chicago was booming. The population rose from 350 in 1833 to nearly 300,000 by 1870. Soon, Chicago was the center of a busy railroad network between the east and west. Then the city went up in smoke and flames!

▲ The Great Chicago Fire

The Lantern

No one really knows what started the Great Chicago Fire of October 8–10, 1871. A drought made the land very dry, so many things could have caused the blaze. A story about Mrs. O'Leary's cow kicking over a lantern was made up by a reporter. Some even think a meteor shower might have sparked the blaze.

Whatever the cause, the gusts that give the "Windy City" its nickname spread flames from a barn at 137 DeKoven Street across miles. The fire burned for two days. Afterward, 300 people were dead; one out of three people had lost their homes; and about 17,500 buildings were ruined.

The Skyscraper

After the fire, Mayor Mason formed the Chicago Relief and Aid Society to give food and shelter to the homeless. People from all over the nation donated money and supplies to help rebuild the city. Taller nonwooden buildings were constructed, such as the Home Insurance Building. At 138 feet, it was the world's first steel-frame "skyscraper."

Home Insurance Building ▶

QUICK CHECK

Summarize How did Chicago get destroyed in 1871?

Lesson 4

VOCABULARY

architect p. 217

arboretum p. 218

institute p. 219

millennium p. 219

READING SKILL

Summarize
Copy the chart below. As you read, fill it in with a summary of Illinois today.

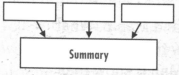

Summary

Illinois Learning Standards
16.A.2b, 16.D.2(W), 17.A.2b

Chicago skyline

Visual Preview

How do people shape Illinois today ?

A Architects in Illinois give the state a special look.

B People in Illinois enjoy their historic and natural places.

C Well-known Illinoisans contribute to the United States.

A THE LOOK OF ILLINOIS

From farms and prairie houses to towers on the Chicago skyline, Illinois greets the twenty-first century with a mix of sights and styles.

Since the great fairs of 1893 and 1933, Chicago has been known as a place for **architects**, or building designers, to show off their work. Daniel Burnham planned out the entire city of Chicago. Some of his buildings still stand in Chicago today.

City Buildings

Visitors are more likely to notice two towers on the skyline. Lake Point Tower, with three curved wings, is shaped like a clover leaf when seen from above. It was the highest apartment building in the world when it was built in 1968.

The Sears Tower, at about 1,450 feet, is the tallest building in the United States. It was designed by Bruce Graham. From its Skydeck, you can see Soldier's Field football stadium.

Soldier's Field is named in honor of World War I heroes. Rebuilt in 2003, it is now home to the Chicago Bears.

Prairie Houses

One of the most famous architects to live in Illinois was Frank Lloyd Wright. He designed homes called "prairie houses," which were inspired by the state's grasslands. Like the Robie House, they have a low roof, overhangs, and an open floor plan and are designed to fit with the land.

QUICK CHECK

Summarize How do the Sears Tower and Wright's prairie houses give Chicago and Illinois a special look?

▼ The Robie House

▼ Frank Lloyd Wright

217

Do you recognize the faces on these pages? These people were either born in Illinois or live here today.

Hillary Rodham Clinton (born 1947)
Clinton spent her childhood in Park Ridge, Illinois. As a lawyer, she worked with a group called the Children's Defense Fund. She was First Lady to President Bill Clinton. In 2000 she was elected to the U.S. Senate.

Barack Obama (born 1961)
Obama moved to Chicago after he graduated from Harvard University. He taught at the University of Chicago Law School. In 2004 he was elected to the U.S. Senate, where he works to improve education, health care, and our environment.

Marlee Matlin (born 1965)
Matlin grew up in Morton Grove, Illinois. She was the youngest actress to win an Academy Award, for her role in *Children of a Lesser God*. She has worked to pass laws so that deaf people can read captions on all TVs, and she helps many charities.

Shel Silverstein (1930–1999)
A poet, cartoon artist, storyteller, and songwriter, "Uncle Shelby" grew up in Chicago. His books, such as *The Giving Tree, Where the Sidewalk Ends*, and *Falling Up*, have given kids hope and encouraged reading.

Robin Williams (born 1951)
A comedian and actor, Williams was born in Chicago. He has starred in dozens of movies and won an Academy Award for *Good Will Hunting*. He runs a charity, the Windfall Foundation, and has performed for American troops overseas.

Oprah Winfrey (born 1954)
Oprah moved to Chicago to host an award-winning TV talk show. She promotes reading with Oprah's Book Club and started the charity Oprah's Angel Network. Oprah is the first African American woman to become a billionaire.

QUICK CHECK

Summarize Besides being born, living, or working in Illinois, what do all of these people have in common?

Check Understanding

1. **VOCABULARY** Write a short letter to a friend that uses all of the words below.

   arboretum   architect   institute
   millenium

2. **READING SKILLS AND STRATEGIES** Summarize Use the graphic organizer on page 216 to help explain how Illinois contributes to the world today.

3. **Write About It** How do architects, artists, and entertainers shape Illinois in different ways?

Summarize

In this unit you will learn about the history of Illinois. Learning how to summarize, or stating the important ideas in a reading paragraph, will help you remember what you learned. A summary gives the main ideas but leaves out minor details. Summarizing will help you understand and remember what you read.

Learn It

- Find the main ideas in a passage. Restate these important points briefly.

- Find important details and combine them in your summary.

- Leave out the details that are not important.

- Now read the passage below and think about how you would summarize it.

Supporting Facts
These facts support the main topic.

Daniel Pope Cook was a newspaper editor. He pushed for Illinois to reach a population of more than 60,000 in order for it to become a state. He had his paper run a story calling for statehood.

Less than a month later, lawmakers in the territory sent the request to Congress. Daniel's uncle, Nathaniel Pope, was a U.S. Congressman. He argued to move the Illinois boundary north to include the area that became Chicago. In April 1818, President Monroe signed the act to move the boundary. The state now had a population of over 60,000. Illinois officially became a state on December 3, 1818.

Main Topic
This is the main topic of the paragraph

Try It

Copy the chart below. Then fill in the chart with your supporting facts from the paragraph on page R10.

Main Topic	→ Supporting Facts
	→
	→
	→

What did you look for to summarize the paragraph?

Apply It

- Review the steps for summarizing in Learn It.
- Read the passage below. Then summarize the passage using a summary chart.

As the white population of Illinois grew, Native Americans were made to sign treaties and move west across the Mississippi River. Black Hawk, a leader of a group of Fox and Sauk, refused to accept the treaties. The U.S. government had already taken more than 26 million acres of land.

Black Hawk rebelled and brought 400 families back to Illinois after hunting season. In 1832 battles broke out between his people and U.S. troops. Black Hawk tried to hold his ground but was defeated at the Bad Axe River.

Geography Handbook

Geography and You

Geography is the study of our Earth and the people who live here. Most people think of geography as learning about cities, states, and countries, but geography is more than that. Geography includes learning about land, such as plains and mountains. Geography also helps us learn how to use land and water wisely.

Did you know that people are part of geography? Geography includes the study of how people adapt to live in a new place. How people move around, how they move goods, and how ideas travel from place to place are also parts of geography.

In fact, geography includes so many things that geographers have divided this information into six elements, or ideas, so you can better understand them.

Six Essential Elements

The World in Spatial Terms: Where is a place located, and what land or water features does this place have?

Places and Regions: What is special about a place, and what makes it different from other places?

Physical Systems: What has shaped the land and climate of a place, and how does this affect the plants, animals, and people there?

Human Systems: How do people, ideas, and goods move from place to place?

Environment and Society: How have people changed the land and water of a place, and how have the land and water affected the people of a place?

Uses of Geography: How does geography influence events in the past, present, and the future?

Five Themes of Geography

You have read about the six elements of geography. The five themes of geography are another way of dividing the ideas of geography. The themes, or topics, are **location**, **place**, **region**, **movement**, and **human interaction**. Using these five themes is another way to understand events you read about in this book.

1. Location

Washington, D. C.

In geography, *location* means an exact spot on the planet. A location is usually a street name and number. You write a location when you address a letter.

2. Place

Seattle, Washington

A *place* is described by its physical features, such as rivers, mountains, or valleys. You would also include the human features, such as cities, language, and traditions, in the description of a place.

3. Region

Florida Everglades National Park

A *region* is a larger area than a place or location. The people in a region are affected by landforms. Their region has typical jobs and customs. For example, the fertile soil of the Mississippi Lowlands helps farmers in the region grow crops.

4. Movement

Los Angeles, California

Throughout history, people have *moved* to find better land or a better life. Geographers study why these movements occurred. They also study how people's movements have changed a region.

5. Human Interaction

Pittsburgh, Pennsylvania

Geographers are interested in how people adapt to their environment. Geographers also study how people change their environment. This *interaction* between people and their environments determines how land is used for cities, farms, or parks.

Dictionary of Geographic Terms

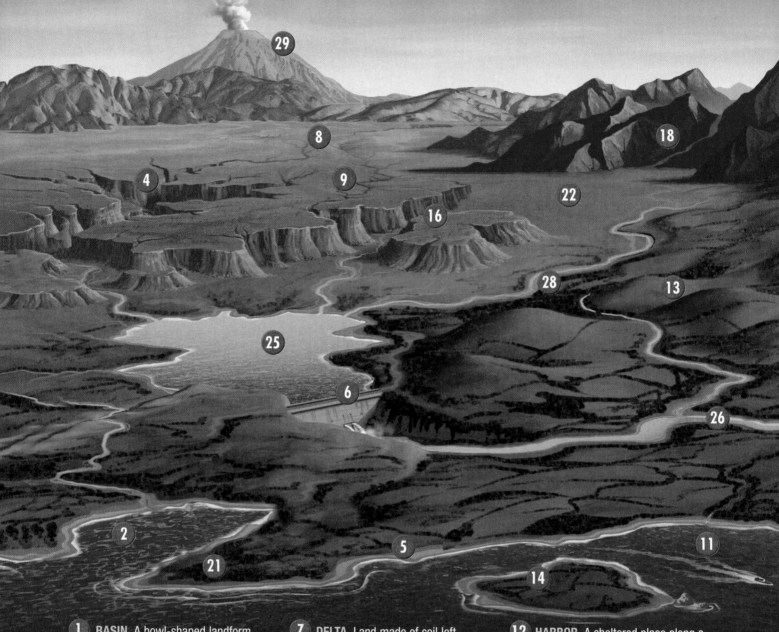

1. **BASIN** A bowl-shaped landform surrounded by higher land

2. **BAY** Part of an ocean or lake that extends deeply into the land

3. **CANAL** A channel built to carry water for irrigation or transportation

4. **CANYON** A deep, narrow valley with steep sides

5. **COAST** The land along an ocean

6. **DAM** A wall built across a river, creating a lake that stores water

7. **DELTA** Land made of soil left behind as a river drains into a larger body of water

8. **DESERT** A dry environment with few plants and animals

9. **FAULT** The border between two of the plates that make up Earth's crust

10. **GLACIER** A huge sheet of ice that moves slowly across the land

11. **GULF** Part of an ocean that extends into the land; larger than a bay

12. **HARBOR** A sheltered place along a coast where boats dock safely

13. **HILL** A rounded, raised landform; not as high as a mountain

14. **ISLAND** A body of land completely surrounded by water

15. **LAKE** A body of water completely surrounded by land

16. **MESA** A hill with a flat top; smaller than a plateau

17 **MOUNTAIN** A high landform with steep sides; higher than a hill

18 **MOUNTAIN PASS** A narrow gap through a mountain range

19 **MOUTH** The place where a river empties into a larger body of water

20 **OCEAN** A large body of salt water; oceans cover much of Earth's surface

21 **PENINSULA** A body of land nearly surrounded by water

22 **PLAIN** A large area of nearly flat land

23 **PLATEAU** A high, flat area that rises steeply above the surrounding land

24 **PORT** A place where ships load and unload their goods

25 **RESERVOIR** A natural or artificial lake used to store water

26 **RIVER** A stream of water that flows across the land and empties into another body of water

27 **SOURCE** The starting point of a river

28 **VALLEY** An area of low land between hills or mountains

29 **VOLCANO** An opening in Earth's surface through which hot rock and ash are forced out

30 **WATERFALL** A flow of water falling vertically

Credits

Illustration Credits : 192: Cody O'Shea. 208: Dan Trush. 224: Wendy Wax.

Photo Credits: All Photographs are by Macmillan/McGraw-Hill (MMH) except as noted below.

Volume 2: iv-v: (bkgd) Forest Preserve District of DuPage County. v: (inset) Ilene MacDonald/Alamy. vi-vii: Adam Jones/Getty Images.

129: Layne Kennedy. 130: (bl) The Granger Collection, New York; (br) Midge Bolt/ boltimaging; (tr) The Granger Collection, New York. 131: (bl) WorldSat International Inc./Science Source/Photo Researchers, Inc.; (br) USFWS, National Wildlife Refuge System; (tl) Corbis/PunchStock; (tr) The Granger Collection, New York. 132: (b) Brand X Pictures/PunchStock; (tr) Eric Meola/Getty Images. 133: (b) Michael Conroy/AP Photos; (tl) Rusty Hill/StockFood America; (tr) Andre Jenny/Alamy Images. 134: (bcr) Ilene MacDonald/Alamy Images; (br) Eric Meola/Getty Images. 137: (t) The Granger Collection, New York. 138: (br) Wind Cave National Park/National Park Service. 138-139: (bkgd) Ilene MacDonald/Alamy Images. 139: (tr) Wind Cave National Park/ National Park Service. 140: (bkgd) Eric Meola/Getty Images. 142: (bcl) Tannen Maury/ The Image Works, Inc.; (bcr) Midwestock; (br) Kevin Fleming/Corbis. 142-143: Lowell Georgia/Corbis. 144-145: (bkgd) Andre Jenny/Alamy Images. 145: (r) Tannen Maury/ The Image Works, Inc. 146: (t) Midwestock. 147: (bkgd) Grant Heilman Photography; (cr) Sean Gallup/Getty Images. 148-149: (b) Kevin Fleming/Corbis. 149: (c) Lowell Georgia/Corbis. 150: (bcl) Bettmann/Corbis; (bcr) Ilene MacDonald/Alamy Images; (bl) Topham/The Image Works, Inc.; (br) AP Photo/Amy Sancetta. 150–151: The Ixtlan Artists Group. 151: (br) Topham/The Image Works, Inc. 152: (t) Bettmann/Corbis. 153: (bl) The Indianapolis Star, Rob Goebel/AP Photos; (tr) Bettmann/Corbis. 154-155: (bkgd) Ilene MacDonald/Alamy Images. 155: (cr) Courtesy of Irene McMullen. 156: (bl) Ionas Kaltenbach/Lonely Planet Images; (tc) The Granger Collection, New York. 156-157: (bkgd) AP Photo/Amy Sancetta. 157: (cr) Bettmann/Corbis; (tr) Michael Kim/Corbis. 158: (c) The Granger Collection, New York. 160: (tl) Ciaran Griffin/Getty Images. 161: Richard Hamilton Smith/CORBIS. 162: (tl) Francisco Villaflor / Alamy; (tr) Don Smetzer / PhotoEdit ; (bl) Calvin Forbes; (br) Courtesy of Jin Lee. 163: (tl) Courtesy of Patrick Marshall; (tr) Glowimages/PunchStock; (br) Associated Press; (bl) Richard Cummins/CORBIS. 164: Kelly-Mooney Photography/Corbis. 165: Danita Delimont / Alamy. 166: (l) Associated Press; (r) Bob Firth. 167: (l) Pilsen Neighbors Community Council; (r) Photo Courtesy Dickson Mounds Museum; (b) SuperStock, Inc. / SuperStock. 168: (l) Journal-Courier / Steve Warmowksi / The Image Works. 170: Jim Wark/Air Photo. 171: David R. Frazier Photolibrary, Inc. / Alamy. 172: (inset) David Muench/CORBIS. 172-173: (b) Forest Preserve District of DuPage County. 173: Royalty-Free/Corbis. 174: Cathy Melloan / PhotoEdit 175: (inset) Bettmann/CORBIS; (bkgd)Associated Press. 176: Vito Palmisano/Getty Images. 177: Bill Stormont/ CORBIS. 178: BILL HOGAN/Newscom. 180: (b) Photos.com/Newscom. 181: (t) Photo by Bob Nichols, USDA Natural Resources Conservation Service; (t) Dave G. Houser/Corbis. 182: Ilene MacDonald / Alamy. 183: Illinois State Archives. 184: (tr) Associated Press; (tl) Courtesy of the Illinois Secretary of State. 185: Associated Press. 186: Associated Press. 187: Jeff Greenberg / Alamy. 188: SuperStock, Inc. / SuperStock. 192: Royalty-Free/Corbis. 193: Scott Olson/Getty Images. 194: (tl) The Granger Collection, New York; (tr) The Granger Collection, New York; (bl) Courtesy of the Abraham Lincoln Presidential Library; (br) Illinois State Archives. 195: (tr) Imagno/Getty Images; (tl) Bettmann/Corbis; (br) Scott B. Rosen; (bl) John Zich/Corbis. 196: The Granger Collection, New York. 197: Jim Wark/Air Photo. 198-199: (b) North Wind / North Wind Picture Archives. 199: (cr) Associated Press; (tc) North Wind / North Wind Picture Archives. 200: (bcl) The Granger Collection, New York; (bcr) Courtesy of the Abraham Lincoln Presidential Library. 201: (tr) POPPERFOTO / Alamy; (bcr) North Wind / North Wind Picture Archives. 202: (tcr) Collection of The New-York Historical Society. 202-203: (b) Bettmann/CORBIS. 203: (tcr) CORBIS. 204: Bettmann/CORBIS. 205: (bc) Underwood & Underwood/CORBIS; (tr) The Granger Collection, NY. 206: (b) Chicago History Museum /Chicago Daily News; (tcr) Bettmann/CORBIS. 207: (cr) Bettmann/CORBIS; (t) Associated Press. 208: (t) CORBIS; (tcr) CORBIS. 208-209: (b) Bettmann/CORBIS; 210: (b) Bettmann/ CORBIS; 211: (b) The New Students' Reference Work; (inset) CORBIS; (br) Bettmann/CORBIS.213: (tc) Swim Ink 2, LLC/CORBIS. 214: (b) Associated Press. 216: Adam Jones/Getty Images. 217: (inset) Associated Press; (bcr) Bibikow,Walter /Index Stock/Jupiter Images. 218: (tr) Richard Hamilton Smith/CORBIS; (bcl) Robert Holmes/CORBIS; (tcl) Richard Day / Daybreak Imagery; (bcr) Richard Hamilton Smith/CORBIS. 219: (inset) James Lemass / SuperStock; (inset) David Davis Photoproductions / Alamy.220: tcl) SZENES JASON/CORBIS SYGMA; (bcl) Getty Images; (tr) Lucy Nicholson/Reuters/Corbis; (br) Jeff Albertson/CORBIS; (tr) LOS ANGELES DAILY NEW/CORBIS SYGMA. 221: Associated Press

ACKNOWLEDGMENTS

Grateful acknowledgment is given to the following authors and publishers. Every effort has been made to trace the ownership of all copyrighted material and to secure the necessary permissions to reprint these selections. In the case of some selections for which acknowledgment is not given, extensive research has failed to locate the copyright holders.